GOVERNMENT REGULATION OF THE RAILROADS

Fighting Unfair Trade Practices in America

David Chiu

ROSEN CLASSROOM
PRIMARYSOURCE
Rosen Classroom Books & Materials
New York

Special thanks to my family and friends

Published in 2006 by The Rosen Publishing Group, Inc.
29 East 21st Street, New York, NY 10010

First Edition

Library of Congress Cataloging-in-Publication Data

Chiu, David.
Government regulation of the railroads : fighting unfair trade practices in America / by David Chiu.
   p. cm. — (The Progressive movement 1900–1920: efforts to reform America's new industrial society)
Includes bibliographical references and index.
ISBN 1-4042-0190-4 (lib. bdg.)
ISBN 1-4042-0849-6 (pbk. bdg.)
6-pack ISBN 1-4042-6188-5
1. Railroads and state—United States—History—Juvenile literature.
I. Title. II. Series: Progressive movement.
HE2757.C47 2004
385'.0973'09041—dc22

2004000752

Manufactured in the United States of America

On the cover: Top: President Theodore Roosevelt, circa 1906. Bottom: Oregon railroad locomotive, 1906.

Photo credits: Cover, p. 12 Library of Congress Prints and Photographs Division; pp. 5, 22 © Corbis; pp. 7, 8 (right), 13 National Archives; p. 8 (left) Private Collection/The Bridgeman Art Library; p. 15 Library of Congress Geography and Map Division; p. 17 Minnesota Historical Society; pp. 18, 20 Wisconsin Historical Society; p. 25 © K.J. Historical/Corbis; p. 26 © Bettmann/Corbis.

Designer: Les Kanturek; Editor: Mark Beyer; Photo Researcher: Amy Feinberg

Contents

Chapter One

The Growth of the American Railroad

The Progressive movement started with a common need to solve many of society's problems. In politics, the public was fed up with dishonesty in city and state government. The rich didn't pay their fair share of taxes. They hid most of their property as stocks and bonds. Women couldn't even vote. Reform efforts forced local governments to act honestly. They also led to the direct election of U.S. senators and to women's right to vote.

On a social level, there was poverty in the cities. People worked in poor and dangerous conditions. Reformers helped start settlement houses so the poor could improve themselves. They inspired new laws for the public good, including worker safety, fair pay, and food inspection.

The main cause for society's problems was the fast industrialization of America. Factory work paid better

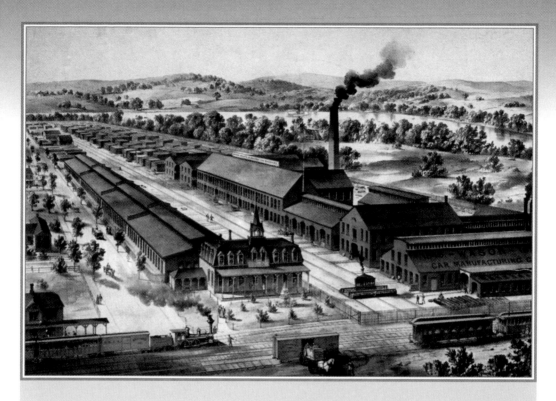

Towns built up around factories, like this one in Springfield, Massachusetts, in 1872. The fast-growing cities helped America change into a wealthy nation. Workers did not share in this wealth. Their wages were low and their living conditions poor.

wages than farm life. People moved into the cities. Pay was still low, and the cost of living was high. Life in the cities became dangerous.

Industry was important to the country's fast growth, however. People depended on companies such as the railroads to make a living. These large companies grew and made a few men rich. But some companies used dishonest ways to stay powerful. Their growth and corruption upset many people. Americans wanted the government to regulate, or control, businesses. Regulation during the Progressive movement changed the ways railroads ran their businesses.

Between the 1860s and the 1920s, the railroad was the fastest and easiest way of moving goods and people. People used railroads to travel across the country in days instead of months. Railroads also opened new markets for farmers and businesses. The railroads employed thousands of people to build the machines and run the lines.

British engineer Richard Trevithick invented the steam locomotive in 1803. American industrialists saw a new form of transportation that could also make them rich. The American railroad industry was born. Major trade states, such as New York, Massachusetts, Pennsylvania, and South Carolina, were the first sites of construction between the 1830s and 1850s. From there, rail lines connected to other cities, such as Chicago, St. Louis, and Memphis.

The promise of gold and new lands caused demand for easier access to the West. So the U.S. government decided that the railroads should connect the East and West Coasts. In 1862, Congress passed the Pacific Railroad Act.

The joining of the transcontinental railroad is celebrated in this picture taken at the Promontory, Utah, site in 1869. People and goods now got from the East and West Coasts in days rather than months.

It gave two companies—the Union Pacific and the Central Pacific Railroads—the right to lay down tracks. When the transcontinental railroad was completed in 1869, America had a rail line crossing the nation.

The railroad became America's first big business. Construction greatly increased in the last half of the

Newspaper cartoons like this one *(left)* showed the power of railroad industrialists such as Cornelius Vanderbilt. Vanderbilt's power over rail transportation cheated business owners and farmers out of money by charging them high rates to use the rail system.

nineteenth century. In 1860, there were 30,000 miles (48,280 kilometers) of track. By 1916, there were 254,000 total track miles (408,773 km). The railroad companies made money, and businessmen saw them as attractive investments. Shipping giant Cornelius

Vanderbilt bought the Hudson River Railroad in 1865. He then combined it with his New York Central Railroad to form a line that connected New York City and Buffalo. It gave Vanderbilt a monopoly (total control) over an important trade route in the Northeast.

Businessmen battled for ownership of the railroads. Sometimes businessmen used corrupt practices to get what they wanted. As co-owner of the Erie Railroad, Jay Gould sold phony stocks to keep his company away from Vanderbilt. He used the Erie stock for his own private use and made millions of dollars. Gould also paid lawmakers to make his dealings look legal. His dishonesty led him to be forced out of the Erie Railroad. The company was left in ruins. Its employees lost their jobs.

Financial leaders continued to buy railroad companies for control over important routes, to cut costs, and to destroy competition. Some rival railroads secretly joined together to set prices. Railroads gave special rebates or discounts to favorite shippers. Free passes were given to lawmakers to gain political favors. The businessmen who used ruthless methods to make themselves rich were called "robber barons."

John D. Rockefeller, the founder of the powerful Standard Oil Company, had been described as a robber baron. He

Cornelius Vanderbilt

Cornelius Vanderbilt (1794–1877), nick-named the Commodore, started a ferry service in New York when he was sixteen. He later ran his own steamship company. It carried goods and passengers between Staten Island and New York City. He became a millionaire. Through organized and ruthless ways, he bought and merged railroads in the 1860s. He died at the age of eighty-two, leaving a fortune worth $105 million (worth $1.6 billion today).

used the railroads to his advantage. Because Standard Oil was so successful, Rockefeller convinced the railroads to ship his oil at a low cost. He was given a rebate, while his rivals had to pay more to transport their oil. This drove out his competition and made Standard Oil the biggest oil company in America.

There were no government laws to challenge these unfair practices. The railroad companies had a monopoly in the small market towns that had only one or two lines. Since the companies provided the only rail service available, they could charge high shipping rates. Farmers and small businesses that needed the railroads to ship their goods were angered by this. They were also upset that they had to pay more for short hauls than long ones.

Chapter Two

The Railroads as Big Business

Farmers and merchants saw the railroad companies as greedy monopolies. In the 1870s, farmers in the Midwest banded together to fight the unfair railroad prices. They called themselves the Grangers. The Grangers demanded that their state governments force the railroads to charge fair and equal rates to all companies. They also wanted the railroads to stop making secret rate agreements with the other railroads. They urged a ban on rebates given to the larger shippers over the small ones.

State governments in Illinois and Wisconsin were the first to pass laws that controlled transportation rates. The railroad companies challenged these laws in the United States courts. In 1876, the Supreme Court ruled that any state had the right to control trade that affected the public. Later, the Court changed its decision. In 1886, the Court decided that only the U.S. government

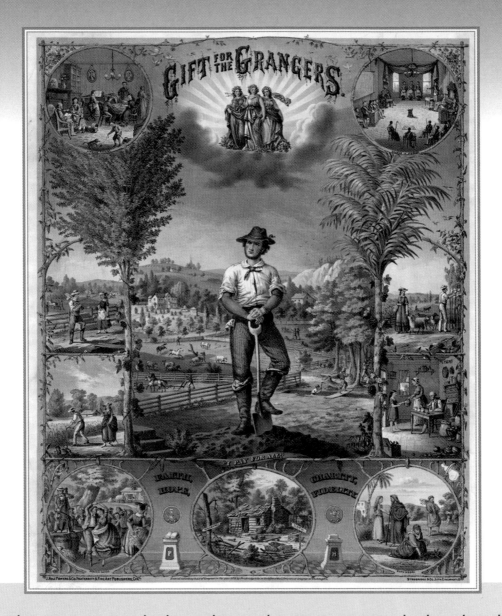

The Grangers worked together in the 1870s against high railroad transportation rates. The group printed posters for its members that showed scenes of farming and farm life.

could control commerce that went beyond state lines.

Railroad owners saw government control, or regulation, as a threat to their power and profits. One railroad president said that the public can either pay the charge "or it can walk." But public demand for reform increased, which led Congress to pass the Interstate Commerce Act in 1887. This law made it illegal for the railroads to charge more for a short haul than a long one. The railroads could not give discounts to shipping companies. The act created the Interstate Commerce Commission (ICC), which would investigate and hear complaints about unfair business practices.

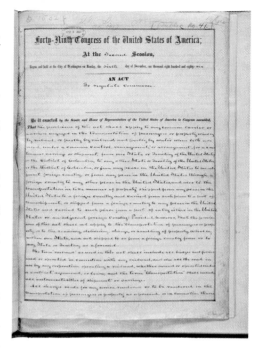

The Interstate Commerce Act was the first law passed to fight unfair railroad rates. It proved to be a weak tool against the powerful railroad owners.

The ICC didn't have powers strong enough to regulate the railroads. Members of the ICC argued with each other on what rates were thought fair or unfair. They were also weakened by the legal system. The Supreme Court favored business interests. It ruled that the ICC had no power to change rates. It also said that only the courts, not the ICC, could punish lawbreakers. The Court decided against the ICC in fifteen cases.

The ICC's weakness allowed railroad companies to continue giving rebates to favored shippers. Meanwhile, competition among railroad companies grew. This happened when two or more lines served the same cities. If one company cut its rates, its competitor did the same. The railroad leaders couldn't agree on the terms because they distrusted each other.

In the 1890s, many railroads began to merge, or combine their companies. Large railroad companies took in smaller rail companies and grew even larger. They did this

J. P. Morgan

J. P. Morgan (1837–1913) was America's leading banker. He lent money to large companies such as U.S. Steel and General Electric. In the early 1890s, Morgan loaned $62 million to the U.S. Treasury. This helped end the country's economic problems. His financial ties with banks, railroads, and insurance companies made him the target of critics. Morgan was also a great collector of art and books. When he died, he left an estate of $80 million (worth $1.2 billion today).

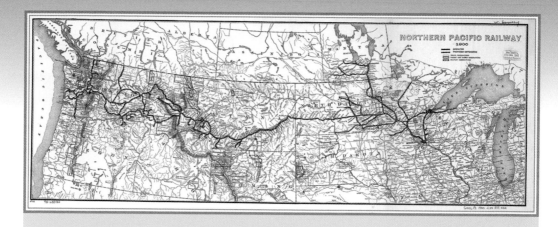

Railroad routes reached across the United States. This map shows the Northern Pacific Railway company's routes through the northern United States. People, businesses, and farmers relied on the railroads to help them travel and transport goods to market. The railroad companies used this need to charge high prices.

to gain control over important routes in a part of the country that would drive off their competitors. The public, however, saw mergers as a threat to economic opportunity for all and the beginning of higher rates.

J. P. Morgan built a railroad empire around consolidation. Consolidation is the process of combining companies into a large corporation. In 1901, Morgan's Northern Pacific Railroad merged with two other railroad systems to form the Northern Securities Company. This move gave Morgan and his partners a monopoly over the important railroad lines in the Pacific Northwest.

Chapter Three

Regulating the Railroads

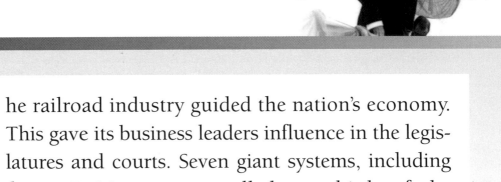

The railroad industry guided the nation's economy. This gave its business leaders influence in the legislatures and courts. Seven giant systems, including one under J. P. Morgan, controlled two-thirds of the nation's rails. The public believed the railroads were beyond government authority. They saw a large amount of wealth and power going into these few large companies. The government did little to oversee the railroads. It believed that all business could regulate itself.

While the 1890s were good times for the rich, they offered little hope for the working class and the poor. Farm prices fell, bankruptcies rose, wages fell, and laborers protested their poor working conditions. Life for the lower class became even harder when the American economy failed in the depression of 1893. This fall in the economy caused thousands of businesses to close,

Railroad companies used their wealth to build more rail lines. These workers building a trestle bridge in Minnesota were paid low wages by rail companies. Millions of people were without work during the early 1890s. Jobs were scarce, and people were willing to work for less pay.

including 156 railroads. A quarter of the United States workforce was unemployed. The farmers, small businesses, and the lower class blamed the railroads and big business for their problems.

In the 1890s, the railroads' power was being challenged during a time of political, social, and economic reform. The

Farmers brought their produce to market for sale and transport using railroads. By the mid-1890s, Progressives were fighting to get fair treatment for farmers from the powerful railroads.

Progressive movement began with a widespread public disapproval of the growth and dishonest ways of the railroads and big business. For the public, control of the railroads by a small number of large corporations meant higher rates. Supporters for reform also wanted improvement for railroad workers. Like so many other American workers, railroad employees worked in poor conditions for little pay. They wanted greater government involvement in the railroads' business practices.

Newspaper and magazine writers influenced public opinion against the railroads. Known also as "muckrakers," they wrote about the social and political abuses of the times. In her articles about the Standard Oil Company, Ida M. Tarbell showed how John D. Rockefeller received special favors from the railroads. These writers brought about greater awareness of the railroad problem and the need to fix it.

Railroad reform had its political supporters. Wisconsin governor Robert La Follette worked to get the legislature to tax the railroads based on property. He also started a railroad regulatory commission. La Follette's efforts at railroad regulation were seen as a model for reform for the whole country. Later, as Wisconsin's senator, La Follette argued that the farmers had no choice but to accept the railroads' high prices because the railroads were a monopoly. He complained that railroads had too much influence on the lawmakers.

The Progressive movement's biggest spokesperson was Theodore Roosevelt. Roosevelt became president in 1901. He supported big business but was also opposed to its arrogance and greed. He knew the American people wanted

Ray Stannard Baker

Ray Stannard Baker (1870–1946) was an American journalist in the early 1900s. A reporter for the *Chicago Record* (1892–1898), he later wrote for *McClure's Magazine* in 1897. Baker wrote about railroad abuses and the problems of black Americans. He supported Progressive reform policies. In 1919, Baker became President Woodrow Wilson's press secretary in Paris. In later years, he wrote a biography of Wilson.

Wisconsin governor Robert "Fighting Bob" La Follette led the early fight against railroad trusts. He wanted to use laws to regulate how railroads did business.

railroad reform. Mail poured in daily to the White House, asking him to fight the railroad business. Roosevelt used his colorful personality to draw people to his reform crusade.

His first target was the Northern Securities Company. J. P. Morgan co-owned this large railroad corporation controlling rail lines in the Northwest. In 1902, Roosevelt ordered the Justice Department to file a lawsuit against the Northern Securities Company using the Sherman Antitrust Act. The Sherman Antitrust Act made it illegal for a single company to control business in one area. In 1904, the Supreme Court agreed with the government and ordered the corporation broken up. From that victory, Roosevelt later filed lawsuits against other large corporations.

Roosevelt pushed for even stronger railroad reform. He worked with Congress on the railroad laws. He went on speaking tours to gain public support. He used Congress

The Sherman Antitrust Act

The Sherman Antitrust Act (1890) declared illegal all combinations of companies that interfered with trade between states and foreign nations. It outlawed trade or commerce monopolies in the United States. Companies that violated the act were ordered to be broken up. President Theodore Roosevelt, who used the act widely, was called a trustbuster.

to carry out his goals. Two major railroad laws were passed during his two terms in office.

The Elkins Act (1903) ended the practice of the railroads giving rebates to their favorite customers. The giving and accepting of rebates was now punishable by fines up to $20,000. The railroads supported this law because they were tired of giving special discounts to large companies like Standard Oil and Carnegie Steel.

Roosevelt wanted a stronger Interstate Commerce Commission with powers to enforce fair rates. The public anti-railroad feeling was so high that a new law easily passed in Congress. The Hepburn Act (1906) increased the size of the ICC and gave it the power to fix rates. Its authority also covered other carriers such as the

President Theodore Roosevelt speaks to a crowd at a political rally. Roosevelt worked against the interests of big business and for the people of the United States. His trust-busting fight against huge railroad companies helped cut fees charged to riders and businesses.

pipelines and sleeping cars. All railroads now had to follow the same bookkeeping practices. They also could no longer give free passes except to their own employees.

Chapter Four

The Effects of Regulation and the Railroad's Decline

N o other president before Theodore Roosevelt had been more active in railroad regulation. Under his leadership, reform became a national campaign. This gave energy to the Progressive movement. It continued through the administrations of the next two presidents.

William Howard Taft succeeded Roosevelt as president in 1909. He continued supporting Progressive programs to fix the railroads. Under his administration, Congress issued the Mann-Elkins Act (1910). It prevented railroads from charging more for a short haul. The ICC's power extended to telephone and telegraph companies. It could stop a new rate increase for 120 days to six months. The railroads now had to prove to the ICC that a rate increase was necessary.

President Woodrow Wilson was also active in business reform. In his first term, the Clayton Antitrust Act (1914) was passed to regulate monopolies. Wilson also wanted to improve the lives of workers. A common workday was twelve hours. Long hours were dangerous to worker safety and health of workers. The Adamson Act (1916) established an eight-hour workday for railroad workers. The act also granted workers overtime pay.

The railroads became the government's main concern when America entered World War I (1914–1918) in 1917. Railroads were important in the shipment of troops and supplies for the war effort. However, the nation's railroads were disorganized. They also lacked the number of rail cars needed for the heavy traffic. Because of regulation, the railroads couldn't raise the rates for money spent on repairs and new equipment.

In December 1917, Wilson ordered the government to take over the railroads. The Railroad Administration was created to oversee the rail lines. Reformers were at first happy about the railroads being under government control. However, the Federal Control Act (1918) reversed some of the earlier reform laws. The government could control the railroads for only twenty-one months after the end of the war. It also promised to repay the owners for using the railroads. Congress briefly took away the rate-making powers of the ICC and gave them to the Railroad Administration.

Following the end of World War I, the government returned the railroads back to their owners through the Transportation Act (1920). It gave the ICC more power to fix rates. It created a Railway Labor Board to handle labor disputes. The ICC allowed railroad companies to combine if they promised good service. Reformers were disappointed that the act allowed mergers.

The Progressive movement faded after the end of the war. In the 1920s, Americans were tired of government involvement in society. Reform was pushed aside for a return to simpler and peaceful ways to run the government. The new government of the 1920s favored industry. It used measures such as raising tariffs to promote American business. As a result, the economy grew throughout the decade.

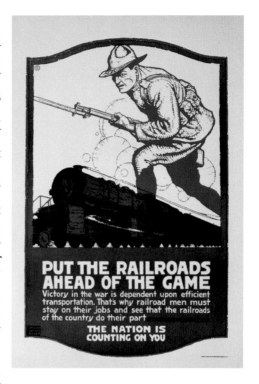

PUT THE RAILROADS AHEAD OF THE GAME

Victory in the war is dependent upon efficient transportation. That's why railroad men must stay on their jobs and see that the railroads of the country do their part

THE NATION IS COUNTING ON YOU

During World War I, the federal government took over the running of the railroads in the United States. The government did not want any problems with moving soldiers and supplies. Both needed to get around the country to ports from which they were shipped to Europe.

The railroad transportation business became less powerful with the use of cars and trucks. This truck transported beef ready for market. It kept the meat cool with its own refrigeration system.

The railroads couldn't enjoy these new times. Years of strict regulation led to their slow decline. The railroads lacked the money to improve themselves because they weren't able to raise rates under the ICC. They faced heavy competition from new forms of transportation: automobiles, trucks, and airplanes. Railroads suffered a decrease in freight and passenger business. They lost their

The Clayton Antitrust Act

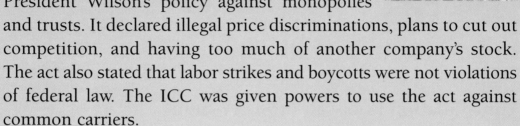

The Clayton Antitrust Act (1914) was a part of President Wilson's policy against monopolies and trusts. It declared illegal price discriminations, plans to cut out competition, and having too much of another company's stock. The act also stated that labor strikes and boycotts were not violations of federal law. The ICC was given powers to use the act against common carriers.

important position in the nation's economy. The government no longer supported them as it had in the past.

Important lessons came out of railroad regulation. The news of railroad abuses was so widespread that it created popular interest in reform. Before the 1900s, the government followed a hands-off policy in the railroads' business. In the Progressive Era, the federal government became directly involved in their affairs. Business was now responsible for providing fair and quality service for everyone. The government had the power to make the rules when a business affected the public welfare. Railroads became the first industry under government regulation and set the example for future reforms in business.

Glossary

commerce (KAH-mers) The buying and selling of goods and services to make money.

Congress (KON-gres) The government body that makes laws.

consolidation (kun-sah-luh-DAY-shun) The act of combining two or more companies into a new one.

corporation (kor-puh-RAY-shun) A business or firm.

corrupt (kuh-RUPT) Dishonest.

enforce (en-FORS) To make sure the law is obeyed.

haul (HAWL) Something that is being transported; a load.

industry (IN-dus-tree) Business.

legislature (LEH-jis-lay-chur) A group of people who make the laws for the state or the nation.

merger (MUR-jer) A combination of two or more corporations.

monopoly (muh-NAH-puh-lee) A company or group of companies that has complete control over a service to the community; the complete control of a product or service for sale to the community.

muckraker (MUK-rayk-er) A name for a writer who exposes political, economic, and social problems.

rebate (REE-bayt) A discount from a payment or bill.

reform (rih-FORM) To improve or to put an end to a wrong.

regulate (REHG-yoo-layt) To control or manage.

regulation (rehg-yoo-LAY-shun) The act of controlling or managing.

robber baron (RAH-ber BEHR-en) Any businessman who became rich through questionable or dishonest ways.

route (ROOT) A road, course, or way of travel from one place to another.

tariff (TAR-rif) A tax placed on something imported from another country.

Web Sites

Due to the changing nature of Internet links, the Rosen Publishing Group, Inc., has developed an online list of Web sites related to the subject of this book. This site is updated regularly. Please use this link to access the list:

http://www.rosenlinks.com/pmnhnt/gorr

Primary Source Image List

Page 5: Print of the Charles R. Wason Manufacturing Company of Springfield, Massachusetts, by D. Parsons, 1872.

Page 7: Photo of the joining of transcontinental railroad tracks at Promontory, Utah, 1869. Currently housed at the National Archives, Washington, D.C.

Page 8 (left): Editorial cartoon titled *The Modern Colossus of Rail Roads* in *Puck*, 1879.

Page 8 (right): Portrait of Cornelius Vanderbilt, circa 1863. Currently housed at the National Archives at College Park, Maryland.

Page 12: Print for Granger members showing scenes of farm life, by J. Hale Powers & Co., circa 1873. Currently housed at the Library of Congress, Washington, D.C.

Page 13: The Interstate Commerce Act, 1887. Currently housed at the National Archives, Washington, D.C.

Page 15: Map of the Northern Pacific Railway Company, 1900. Created by the L. L. Poates Engineering Company. Currently housed at the Library of Congress, Washington, D.C.

Page 18: Photograph of Milwaukee, Wisconsin, farmer's market, by Henry Hamilton Bennett. Currently housed at the Wisconsin Historical Society, Madison, Wisconsin.

Page 20: Political cartoon depicting Wisconsin governor Robert La Follette, by McWhorter, 1906. Currently housed at the Wisconsin Historical Society, Madison, Wisconsin.

Page 25: Government poster titled "Put the Railroads Ahead of the Game," by Ernest Hamlin Baker, circa 1915.

Index

About the Author

David Chiu is an author and freelance writer living in New York City.